GW00854801

Wonderful Christmas Decorations

DIY Festive Felt Christmas Ornaments

© 2020 All rights reserved

Table of Content

Introduction

I cannot believe that Christmas is already just around the corner! Christmas is my favorite time of year. I love the hustle and bustle, the family, the surprises and most of all I love the decor! Bring on all of the Christmas!

Every year when the stores start rolling out their Christmas decorations I immediately start itching to get mine up as well!

One of the things I love about decorating my own home for Christmas is creating DIY projects and pieces. My home is Farmhouse Modern and I love to make fun decor pieces to add to the existing decor of the home.

These little felt Christmas ornaments are so easy to make yourself, but look so elegant and lovely on the tree!

They make perfect handmade gifts, or as a way to add a personal touch to your own Christmas tree.

EASY DIY FELT CHRISTMAS BUNTING AND ORNAMENTS

I am currently loving felt and knew that I had to make something fun so this year I made an easy DIY project that is just a perfect accent. I originally started with a bunting but loved it so much I also made some ornaments. These easy DIY felt Christmas Bunting and ornaments took no time at all to make and I just love them!

Supplies

- 1/2 yard of felt

- Embroidery Thread

- Embroidery Needle

- Small Buttons

- Glue Gun

- Pillow Stuffing

- Tree and Star Template

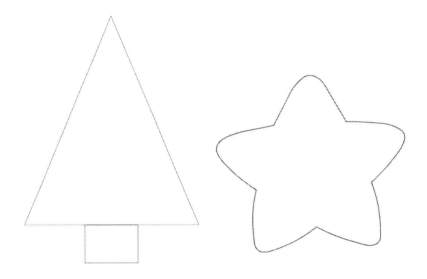

Directions

Trace your desired shape onto your felt. If you are going to make them into "pillows" cute 2 shapes per ornament. Once all of your pieces are cut out, it is time to sew. Using the embroidery thread and needle thread first sew on your buttons. Arrange them how ever you feel best one your front piece of felt.

Once your buttons are sewn on, you will double your shapes and sew them together using a looping pattern along the edge of your ornament.

Be sure that when you are sewing you leave a small opening for the stuffing. Add a small amount of stuffing to each ornament then finish sewing. Repeat for all trees and stars.

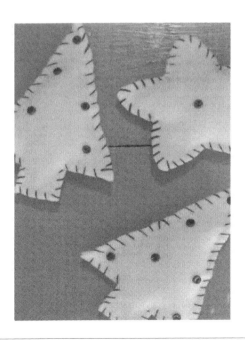

Once your ornaments are complete it is time to glue them onto the ribbon. If you are creating a bunting, measure the space then glue ornaments on. I glued mine from the very top. I tried gluing them in the middle but it tipped over. For tree ornaments, create a small loop with your ribbon for hanging and glue to the back.

This fun project is perfect for the fireplace mantle or even a fun window!

I am telling you friends, creating these DIY Felt Christmas bunting and ornaments were so easy the kids could help!

FELT CHRISTMAS TREE ORNAMENT

I love handmade ornaments and I've waited a whole year to share these little firs. It started with an email from my mom last fall after she returned from a local gardening shop she and her husband frequent. The link was to a darling multicolored felt stack Christmas tree pair, something for the mantel, cute as all get out

Supplies

- felt, colors are up to you

- a strip of felt, 1/2 inch wide by 2 1/2 inches long

- **printable size guide**

- embroidery thread (or regular thread)

- needle

- glue gun

- gold paint (to paint tree top square 'star')

Directions

First, cut all the felt squares, the amount and size according to the printable guide.

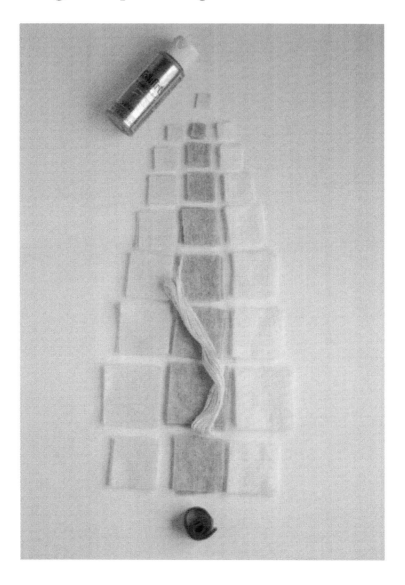

Then start stacking them up. Begin with the bottom (4 – 1 3/4") and stack through to the top (6 – 1/2"). I arranged my colors so none of the same were next to each other but again, that part is up to you. Run a needle and thread through the center of each of the stacks until all are strung.

Add a dot of glue to the brown piece of felt and wrap it around the thread and itself, adding another dot of glue to keep the strip in place.

To finish up, add a dot of glue to one of the two star squares and sandwich them together, making sure to secure the end of the thread in between the pieces. This step not only holds the stack in place but is where the hanging loop is created. Then arrange the felt pieces, off setting the pieces from each other.

Then hang them and smile at their adorableness.

Enjoy!!!

FELT COFFEE CUP ORNAMENTS

This Christmas, I wanted to give my friends a little token of friendship to show them I'm thankful they're in my life and I enjoy the time we spend together. Since I'd need more of whatever I bought, I needed to find something inexpensive but meaningful at the same time. Here's what I came up with.

Supplies

- Felt {red, white, light brown}
- Red and white baker's twine or other string

- Scissors

- Green fabric paint
- Red thread

- Sewing needle

- Hot glue gun and glue sticks

- Craft glue

- Fine glitter

Directions

Step 1: Cut your felt pieces. For each ornament, you will need two red cup shapes, one white lid, and a brown cup sleeve. I freehanded a pattern for mine.

Step 2: Hand stitch the two cup pieces together around both sides and the bottom.

Step 3: Cut a piece of twine and tie it into a knot.

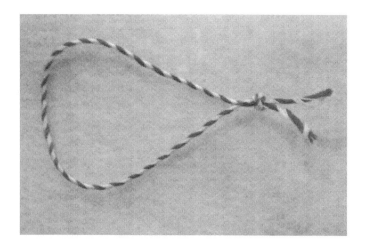

Step 4: Open the top of the cup and put a dab of hot glue inside. Insert the knotted end of the twine and glue shut.

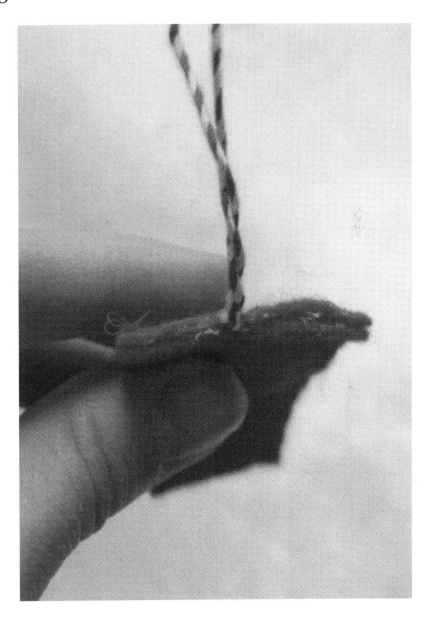

Step 5: Use fabric paint to add a small green heart or whatever you like to the cup sleeve. Then, glue the sleeve and the lid to the cup.

Step 6: Spread some glue on the lid and sprinkle with fine glitter! Why? Glitter makes everything better!!

Just a note, I strongly advise following the steps in order and **putting your fabric paint on BEFORE you glue everything together**. Because if you try painting after it's all glued, something like this might happen. Just saying. And then it will be practically impossible to get that "cup sleeve" off since you hot glued it together and hot glued felt sticks together in a big way. Not that I know or anything...

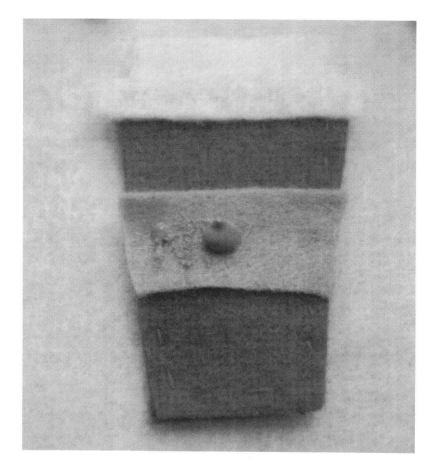

Felt Hot Cocoa Ornament

Now I don't have the snow – but I still love to have the fire, watch the best Christmas movie ever and have a cup of cocoa. I can just do it and watch the ocean out my window. Much better.

This little ornament is perfect to remind me of those cold – or not so cold – winter nights!!

Isn't it cute? I was in Target the other day and saw these cute pj's in the girls section that had a smiling mug of cocoa and two little cute marshmallows on the front. I thought the idea would be perfect for a fun little ornament!

Supplies

- Felt – blue, brown and white
- Embroidery floss – matching colors
- tiny bit of pink paint
- thin batting
- floral wire
- Pattern

Directions

Start by cutting out all your pieces out of felt.

Place the cocoa piece over the top mug piece, according to the placement on the pattern. Sew the cocoa to the mug using a blanket stitch. This is super easy and not scary at all. Start by bringing your needle up about 1/4" below the edge of the brown felt.

Repeat this last step again to start forming the blanket stitch.

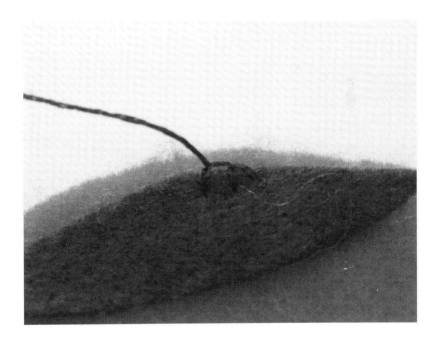

Sew all the way around the cocoa piece until you come back to the beginning. For the last stitch, loop it through the first stitch to make the thread lay flat.

Sew the eyes and mouth onto this piece by using small stitches and following the pattern placement. Fill the eyes in with long straight stitches.

Oh so cute!!
Cut out a layer of thin batting the same pattern as the mug and layer it between the mug front and back. Sew together the mug pieces beginning with the inside of the mug handle. Use a blanket stitch, making sure the batting doesn't show between.

Make faces on two of the marshmallow pieces according to the pattern placement. Use french knots for the eyes.
Dab a tiny bit of pink paint on to give them rosy cheeks.

Layer together a marshmallow front and back with a piece of batting between them. Start sewing them together with a blanket stitch about halfway down on the right side. Sew across the top and down the left side about halfway.

Place the marshmallow on top of the cocoa section of the mug.

Finish sewing the marshmallow closed, but for the rest of the way around, sew it to the mug as you go.

Repeat for the other Marshmallow.

To make the steam "curls", wrap a piece of wire around a pen or something handy like that. This is my Party Pictionary pen. Yes, this was what was handy.

You never know when you're going to need to draw a random doodle so someone can guess what you drew.

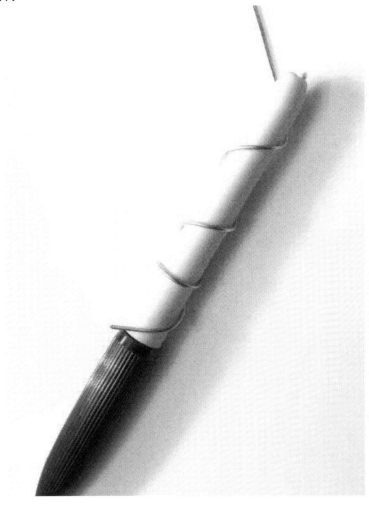

Leave a bit of wire (about 3") on the end straight. Clip the wire.

Feed the straight end of the wire down through the top of one of the marshmallows, between the felt pieces. Force it through the felt in the back just where the mug starts, then feed it into the mug pieces. This will help it stay straight up. You can then bend and adjust the curl they way you want. Repeat with the other marshmallow and another wire curl.

Make a loop with embroidery floss and sew it to the back of the ornament for hanging.

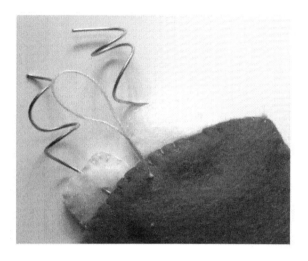

Admire your cute new little ornament!!

Felt Fox Ornament

I am still doing some last minute Christmas prep and decided I wanted to make ornaments for some of my coworkers. I came up with this little felt fox pattern and decided to share it with you all. While I used needle and thread to put mine together, you can also use hot glue or fabric glue if you want to whip up multiples of these for gifts yourself and save time!

Supplies

- Fox ornament pattern
-
  Two colors of felt (I used red and cream, you can change up your foxes to be any color you like)
-
  Scissors
-
  Pen
-
  Needle and thread
-
  Buttons in various sizes
-
  Polyfil or other soft stuffing
-
  Ribbon, thread or cord for hanging the ornament

Directions

Start by printing the fox ornament pattern. It comes in two sizes, so you can make a whole family of foxes if you like (or use the pattern that fits your tree best). Trace the patterns onto your felt and cut out the pieces (you will need two of the larger head piece and one face piece for each ornament).

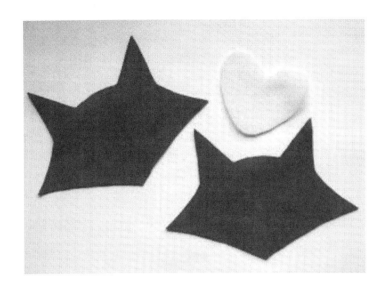

Arrange the face piece onto the head, move around until you are satisfied. Felt tends to stick to itself a bit, but feel free to pin your face pieces in place before sewing together (or just use fabric or hot glue to put these together).

Select buttons in a color and size you like. Place them onto the face piece and glue them down or sew them on. Once you have this piece completed, you can layer together the two head pieces and begin sewing or gluing those together (make sure to leave a hole for adding stuffing). Before sewing up the top of the head, I add in a ribbon or some metallic cord to use to hang my ornaments from the Christmas tree. I used a blanket stitch to sew my pieces together, but you can use any stitch you are comfortable with (or again, glue is great and makes this super fast and easy--the kids can even help!).

Hang your finished product on the tree or give these as gifts (they are super cute on packages instead of bows!)

Felt Calcifer Ornament

Let's make your Christmas on fire!!!

Supplies

- The template

- Felt (gold, orange, brown, white)

- Embroidery floss (orange, brown)

- Polyester stuffing

- Ribbon or string

- Sewing needle

- Pins

- A black permanent marker

- Scissors

- A pen/chalk

- Hot glue sticks and a hot glue gun

First you will need to print out the template.

Cut out all of the template pieces. (the top piece is for placement reference)

Trace the log piece onto your brown felt. Flip the template piece and trace again to create a front and back log piece. Cut out both pieces.

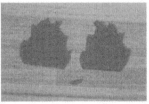

Trace the larger flame piece onto orange felt. Flip the template and trace again to create a front and back. Also trace the mouth piece. Cut out all 3 pieces.

Trace the smaller flame piece onto gold felt and cut out.

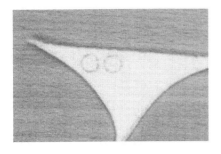 

Trace 2 eye pieces onto white felt and cut out.

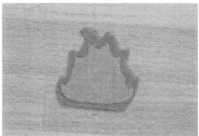

Hot glue the gold flame piece onto one of the larger orange flame pieces. Use the finished Calcifer from the template for placement assistance.

Glue the eye and mouth pieces in place.

 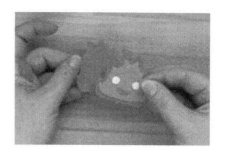

Match up the front and back orange flame pieces right sides out and pin in place.

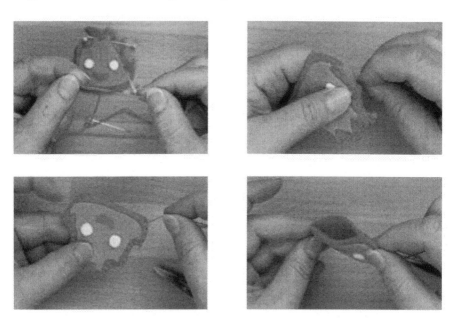

Cut a length of your orange embroidery floss and separate to use 3 strands. Thread sewing needle. Start at one of the lower bottom corners securing your thread and begin to work around the flame using a blanket stitch. Stop and secure thread at opposite bottom corner leaving the bottom of the flame open.

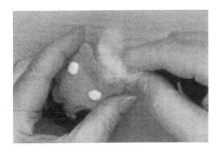 

Stuff your flame to desired firmness.

Sandwich a small section of the lower flame pieces between the 2 log sections and pin in place.

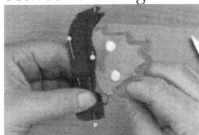 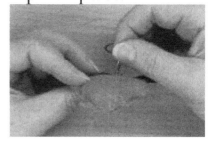

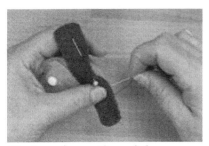 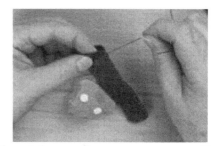

Cut a length of brown embroidery floss, separate 3 strands and thread your sewing needle.

Starting at one end of the log, secure your thread to the upper corner of the longer side that has the flame pieces attached. Blanket stitch until you get to the flame then take small stitches through all sections of felt (log and flame pieces). Continue to blanket stitch once you pass the flame until you reach the lower edge of the long side of the log, opposite to where you started. This leaves the end of the log open for stuffing. Leave excess thread and needle attached to close opening once stuffed.

Push stuffing into the end of the log using a pen/ thin tool until desired firmness is reached.

Sew end of log closed using blanket stitch. Secure thread and cut off excess.

Cut a length of ribbon and overhand knot ends together to create a loop.

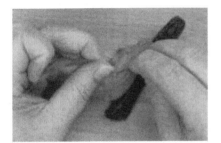

Sew or glue ribbon onto the back of the flame for hanging.

Using a black permanent marker, draw on pupils and wood grain using the template for reference.

Now you have your finished Calcifer ornament!

Printed in Great Britain
by Amazon

70921687R00031